Just the Facts

Meningitis

Kristina Routh

Heinemann Library
Chicago, Illinois

Customer Service   888–454–2279
Visit our website at www.heinemannlibrary.com

Produced by Monkey Puzzel Media
Designed by Jane Hawkins
Consultant: Beverley Corbett, Educational and Training Manager, Meningitis Trust
Orignated by Ambassador Litho Ltd
Printed and bound in China by South China Printing Company

08 07 06 05 04
10 9 8 7 6 5 4 3 2 1

Library of Congress Cataloging-in-Publication Data
 A copy of the cataloging-in-publication data for this title is on file with the Library of Congress.
Meningitis/ Kristina Routh
ISBN 1-4034-5146-X

Acknowledgments
The author and publishers are grateful to the following for permission to reproduce copyright material: Alamy pp. 4 (Robert Harding Picture Library), 27 (Penny Tweedie), 37 top (Phototake Inc./Yoav Levy), 51 (David Young-Wolff); Corbis pp. 10 (Reflections/Jenny Woodcock), 11 (Bob Krist); Hulton Archive p. 7 (Fred Ramage); Imaging Body p. 20; Meningitis Trust pp. 14, 17, 41; Panos Pictures p. 26 (Betty Press); PA Photos pp. 29 (EPA), 37 bottom (Owen Humphreys), 46 (David Kendal); Science Photo Library pp. 1 (James Prince), 8 (Simon Fraser/Royal Victoria Infimary, Newcastle-upon-Tyne), 15 (Gary Parker), 16 (Dr Kari Lounatmaa), 19 (James Prince), 22 (Dr P Marazzi), 30 (John Cole), 32 (Simon Fraser/Royal Victoria Infirmary, Newcastle-upon-Tyne), 33 (TEK Image), 34 (Larry Mulvehill), 40 (Mauro Fermariello), 43 (Adam Hart-Davis), 49 (Mike Miller); Topham Picturepoint pp. 13 (Image Works), 23 (Image Works/Bob Daemmrich), 24 (Image Works/Larry Kolvoord), 28 (Image Works/Bob Daemmrich), 39 (Image Works/Ellen Senisi), 44 (Photri); Wellcome Library, London p. 6.

Cover photograph by: main image: Science Photo Library/ James Prince; Science Photo Library/ Dr. Kari Lounatmaa

Contents

Introducing Meningitis

Meningitis occurs all over the world; it is truly a global disease. Most people have read newspaper stories about meningitis or seen television programs about it. Meningitis is often referred to as a "killer" disease, and one that can strike unexpectedly, especially in babies and children.

As is often the case, the real facts are more complicated. It is true that meningitis can kill, but in most cases those who suffer from it recover. The disease can leave a person with serious and disabling aftereffects, such as deafness or epilepsy. Yet this does not happen in most cases.

A severe headache is one of the most common symptoms of meningitis.

Meningitis is much more common in babies and children, but it can also affect healthy teenagers and adults. People who have a weak immune system, perhaps because of disease or old age, are also at risk.

So what is meningitis?

Meningitis is a serious infection that affects the delicate membranes covering the brain and spinal cord. Among other things, it may cause headaches, vomiting, fever, and confusion. In the most severe cases of the disease, the individual becomes so ill that he or she must be taken to the hospital immediately to receive life-saving treatment.

Many different micro organisms can cause meningitis. Most cases are caused by viruses or a few particular types of bacteria. Although viral meningitis can sometimes be quite serious, the bacterial form of the disease is most likely to cause severe problems.

Bacterial meningitis is particularly likely to be harmful when it is accompanied by septicemia - infection of the blood (see page 14).

Education

In many cases, the danger with meningitis comes when it is not recognized early enough. People have died who might have been saved if they had been given treatment sooner. Health departments and charitable meningitis organizations work hard to publicize the signs and symptoms of meningitis so that people will know when to seek medical help. These organizations also provide information to the media so that the reporting of cases of meningitis can be more balanced and informative, and less alarming.

"Meningitis and septicemia are life-threatening diseases. Knowing the signs and symptoms of meningitis and septicemia, and acting quickly to get medical help, can save lives."

(The Meningitis Research Foundation, United Kingdom)

Meningitis over the Years

One of the most important types of meningitis – meningococcal meningitis (see page 16) – was first described in 1805 by Gaspard Vieusseux, a doctor in Geneva, Switzerland. Unlike some other infectious diseases – such as tuberculosis, which had been documented for thousands of years – there was very little description of meningitis before the beginning of the 19th century.

Epidemics

From the beginning of the 1800s, epidemics (large outbreaks) of meningococcal meningitis began to occur. From 1806 to 1816, there were many cases in the United States, especially in New England. The first book about meningococcal meningitis – or "spotted fever" as it was known – was written by Elisha North of Connecticut and was published in 1811.

As the 19th century progressed, the disease began to appear in many different countries. Europe was badly affected, with many deaths occurring in countries such as France, Italy, and Germany. Between 1854 and 1861, 4,100 people died in Sweden alone and many more were left in poor health. By 1875 reports of meningococcal meningitis had started to come from Africa, Asia, and Australia. The bacterium that cause this type of meningitis – *Neisseria meningitidis* (or meningococcus) – was identified in 1887 by Anton Weichselbaum of Vienna, Austria.

Scientist Anton Weichselbaum identified the bacterium that causes one type of meningitis.

6

Epidemics of meningococcal meningitis have been particularly associated with times of war, when there are large-scale movements of people and many are forced to live crowded together in poor conditions. The disease was widespread during the time of the Civil War (1861–1865), and there were epidemics during both World War I (1914–1918) and World War II (1939–1945).

Treatment

Before antibiotics were introduced in the 1930s, little could be done to treat meningitis. Over three-quarters of all people who got meningococcal meningitis died, and many more were left disabled.

In the late 1930s, the first antibiotics were used against meningitis. Sulfanilamide was given to soldiers in the French Foreign Legion serving in West Africa during an outbreak of the disease. While supplies lasted, the death rate was reduced from 75 percent to 11 percent.

Penicillin, which first became widely used in the 1940s, proved very effective against meningitis. Finally, doctors had a reliable way to combat this terrible disease. And today, in the 21st century, penicillin remains one of the most important antibiotics for treating bacterial meningitis.

The Many Causes of Meningitis

Meningitis is the infection of the meninges, the delicate membranes that cover and protect the brain and spinal cord. There are three layers of membranes: the dura is the tough outer layer, the arachnoid is the middle layer (named for its spider like appearance), and the pia is the inner layer, which is rich in blood vessels. The brain and spinal cord are bathed in a special liquid called cerebrospinal fluid (CSF). This also becomes infected in meningitis.

Once an infection has affected the meninges, it can be difficult for the body to fight it. There are not many defense cells or antibodies in the CSF as there are in the blood. When the body does fight back, it causes inflammation, which may then damage the brain.

brain

This brain scan shows someone with meningitis. The areas highlighted in yellow are patches of inflammation caused by the infection.

spinal cord

Viruses

Many different types of organisms can cause meningitis. The most common are viruses. Viruses are incredibly tiny micro organisms, much too small to be seen under a normal microscope. They are so small that they can even infect bacteria! Viral meningitis is usually less serious than bacterial meningitis – which is lucky because there are no medicines to treat it. Most people with viral meningitis get better after a few weeks.

Bacteria

Bacteria are small organisms that can be seen in the laboratory under a microscope. Taken as a group, they are the second most common cause of meningitis. Bacterial meningitis tends to be more serious than viral meningitis and may even cause death. There may be an associated infection of the bloodstream, known as septicemia, which is usually serious. However, unlike viruses, bacteria can be killed by antibiotics and so treatment is available.

Types of bacterial meningitis

- Pneumococcal meningitis, caused by the bacterium *Streptococcus pneumoniae*
- Meningococcal meningitis, caused by the bacterium *Neisseria meningitidis*
- Hib meningitis, caused by the bacterium *Haemophilus influenzae, type b*

Meningitis can also be caused by some other bacteria, including *Escherichia coli* (*E. coli*), Group B streptococci, salmonella, and *Mycobacterium tuberculosis*, the bacteria responsible for tuberculosis (see page 24).

Other causes

Although meningitis is usually caused by viruses or bacteria, there are some rare cases in which the disease is caused by certain types of fungi or protozoa (see page 25).

How Does Meningitis Spread?

How meningitis spreads depends upon whether viruses or bacteria are causing the disease.

Viral meningitis

Viral meningitis can occur in outbreaks, sometimes at particular times of the year. The viruses that are most likely to cause meningitis can be spread in two main ways:

- Respiratory droplets – tiny drops of saliva or mucus from the nose, which are coughed, sneezed, or even breathed out. These can be breathed in by someone else or may be passed on when shaking hands with an infected person.
- Via feces. The viruses may live in the intestines and get to the hands after an infected person uses the toilet or changes a baby's diaper. If the person does not wash his or her hands properly, the virus may be passed on to another person. This can happen by touching food that someone else will eat. Young children, who may not remember to wash their hands, often pass on viruses in this way.

Bacterial meningitis

The bacteria that can cause bacterial
meningitis often live quite harmlessly
for weeks or months in the lining of
the nose and throat of healthy people.
This is known as colonization. At any
one time, between 10 and 25 percent
of people are colonized in this way.

Occasionally, these bacteria get past
the body's defenses to enter the
bloodstream. Then they may cause
septicemia or travel to the meninges to
cause meningitis – or sometimes both.

Of the types of bacterial meningitis,
only meningococcal meningitis occurs
in outbreaks. Pneumococcal meningitis
and Hib meningitis do not seem to
spread from person to person.

Meningococcal bacteria are fragile and
die quite quickly outside the body.
This means that they can be passed
from person to person through close
contact. Kissing is a well-known way
of passing on these bacteria. Just
being near an infected person when he
or she sneezes or coughs can also
cause infection. This kind of meningitis
usually only spreads within a
community where people spend a lot
of time close together. For example,
there have been outbreaks in schools
and military training camps.

Symptoms of Meningitis

Recognizing meningitis is crucial. In some cases, early treatment may mean the difference between life and death. At first, the symptoms might not be clear, or may seem like those of the flu. But in meningitis, the infected person can become very ill. Symptoms of viral meningitis may be similar to those of bacterial meningitis but are usually not as severe.

Typical symptoms

These symptoms may not appear in any particular order, and some may not appear at all. The illness may develop over several days or sometimes in a few hours. The best-known symptoms of meningitis and meningococcal septicemia that include

- a headache, which is usually severe
- neck stiffness, which may mean the sufferer is unable to touch his or her chin to the chest
- photophobia (an intense sensitivity to bright light)
- drowsiness or confusion; there may even be seizures
- fever; there may be a high temperature, perhaps with cold hands and feet

- vomiting and sometimes diarrhea
- a rash, in which there is septicemia (see page 14)
- joint pain or aching, especially in septicemia.

Sally's story

Sally was fifteen when she developed meningococcal meningitis and septicemia. She recalls, "I couldn't stop vomiting – I thought I had eaten something that had made me ill. I tried to go upstairs but I couldn't get past the first step. My father later said that I was drifting in and out of consciousness. I was so bad that he had to help me get undressed and get into bed. I had a very high temperature, so he tried giving me sponge baths to keep it down. When the doctor came to my house, she immediately noticed two bruises on my upper arm that had just started to appear. She diagnosed meningococcal disease right away and called an ambulance. I was taken to the hospital, the ambulance siren blaring all the way."

Babies and young children

Many cases of meningitis occur in babies and young children, who often do not show the typical symptoms.

Parents who are worried that their baby might have meningitis should look for

- a high-pitched, moaning cry
- fever, perhaps with cold hands and feet
- vomiting
- refusal to eat
- limpness when being picked up
- pale, blotchy skin
- extreme sleepiness
- a rash in which there is septicemia.

Meningitis and meningococcal septicemia require urgent medical attention. Anyone who is in any doubt should see a doctor.

A high temperature is one of the common signs of meningitis.

Types of Meningitis

Blood poisoning

Septicemia is a bacterial infection of the blood, also known as blood poisoning. It is usually a serious and life-threatening condition. Septicemia is included here because the bacteria that cause meningitis may also cause septicemia, sometimes together with meningitis, sometimes alone.

Septicemia is especially likely to occur with infection by meningococci. When someone has both meningococcal meningitis and septicemia, it is commonly called meningococcal disease. It is not known why some people develop meningitis, some develop septicemia, and some develop both.

What happens?

In septicemia, bacteria multiply rapidly within the bloodstream and produce poisons that damage the walls of the blood vessels. Blood can then leak out of the blood vessels into the surrounding tissues. This leakage of blood leads to the major symptoms of septicemia:

- A rash. Blood leaking out into the tissues under the skin causes the distinctive rash that often appears in meningococcal disease (see glass tumbler test below and opposite). The rash starts as tiny red spots, but these soon get larger and turn into purple bruises.
- Raised heart rate. As more and more blood is lost from the bloodstream into the tissues, the heart pumps faster in an attempt to increase the circulation.
- Cold hands and feet. The circulatory system starts to shut down, keeping what blood there is for the vital internal organs rather than for the limbs.

This rash has not faded under the glass. It might be due to meningococcal septicemia (see page 15).

- Multiple organ failure. Eventually, the lack of blood for the vital internal organs causes them to fail and death often follows.

Meningococcal septicemia is a medical emergency. Most deaths from meningococcal disease are a result of the septicemia. Only prompt treatment with antibiotics gives an infected person a good chance of survival.

Intravenous antibiotics are necessary to treat bacterial meningitis.

The glass tumbler test

The glass tumbler test is a simple way to tell if a skin rash could be a result of meningococcal septicemia. The meningococcal rash is non blanching, which means that it does not fade (blanch, or whiten) if pressure is applied to it. Other less harmful rashes will blanch if pressed.

A glass tumbler (or any piece of safe, clear glass) is pressed firmly against the rash. The rash is then viewed through the glass to see if it has whitened, or disappeared. If it is still present, then it might be a result of meningococcal septicemia. Medical attention should be sought immediately.

Meningococcal meningitis

The most common type of bacteria to cause meningitis is known as *Neisseria meningitidis* (or meningococci). These bacteria are found in people througout the world. Up to one quarter of individuals carry them harmlessly in their throats. It is only occasionally that they go on to cause infection, although epidemics can occur and affect many people. Meningococci can cause both meningitis and septicemia.

In many countries, such as the United States and United Kingdom, cases of meningococcal meningitis tend to occur seasonally in the winter and early spring. For some reason, the disease seems to appear in ten to fifteen year cycles, although it never goes away completely.

Meningococcal meningitis and septicemia can affect people of all ages, but is most common in young children and teenagers. Roughly

The bacterium that causes meningococcal meningitis, *Neisseria meningitidis*, is shown here greatly magnified by a powerful electron microscope.

5 to 10 percent of people who get meningococcal disease will die, usually as a result to septicemia. Many people recover completely, but some are left with severe and disabling after effects such as deafness, epilepsy, muscle weakness, or even loss of limbs resulting from amputations.

A dangerous infection

Meningococcal disease can be treated with antibiotics, but even with modern medical treatment it can be a life-threatening infection. It is vital that treatment starts as early as possible.

Types of meningococci

Like many bacteria, meningococci can be divided into several groups, or serogroups. The five groups that are responsible for most of the cases of meningococcal disease around the world today are known as B, C, A, Y, and W-135.

The B and C groups are the most common types found in many developed countries, such as the United States and United Kingdom. There is a vaccine for group C, but none yet for group B, which tends to be more common. Group Y occurs in the United States but is rare in Europe.

The Internet is a good way to find out about the many types of meningitis.

Group A is common in sub-Saharan Africa (where it causes large epidemics), Pakistan, Nepal, and parts of India. W-135 has only recently emerged as an important group. Most of the cases are in Africa, but this group is now spreading to other regions.

Pneumococcal meningitis

Pneumococcal meningitis is caused by bacteria called *Streptococcus pneumoniae* (or pneumococci), which many people carry harmlessly in the back of the nose and throat. They can cause ear and sinus infections, pneumonia, meningitis, and septicemia.

Pneumococci are the second most common cause of meningitis in the United States and United Kingdom. This type of meningitis is not contagious (catching) and does not occur in outbreaks. The symptoms tend to be the same as other types of meningitis but without a rash.

Pneumococcal meningitis has a higher fatality rate and risk of serious after effects, such as deafness and brain damage, than meningococcal disease. In many countries, a vaccine is available for those at greatest risk.

(Opposite) Pneumococcal meningitis is a serious disease, often requiring intensive care in a hospital.

Who gets this disease?

Most cases of pneumococcal meningitis are seen in young children and the elderly. People with a medical condition that lowers their immunity also have a higher risk. They include those who

- do not have a spleen because it has been injured or removed, or have a poorly functioning spleen, such as in sickle cell disorder. (The spleen forms part of the body's immune system.)
- have a long-standing disease of the heart, lungs, kidney, or liver
- have diabetes
- have a head injury or defect in their skull through which the bacteria can spread
- have low immunity because of HIV infection or because they are taking medicines that weaken their immune system
- have cochlear implants– these are mechanical devices implanted in the inner ear to aid hearing. They may allow bacteria to reach the meninges from the ear canal.

Aimee's story

Aimee had always been a happy, healthy baby, so her parents were quite worried when she suddenly seemed sick. Aimee's sister Jackie remembers, "She was restless, whining, and had a high temperature that wouldn't come down." After several trips to the family doctor, Aimee was rushed to the hospital.

Tests showed that Aimee had pneumococcal meningitis. She spent the next two weeks fighting for her life while the doctors and nurses did all they could to treat her. "Everyone in my family and the doctors were unsure whether or not Aimee was going to make it," says Jackie. But Aimee fought hard and survived. She has been left with many medical problems, including epilepsy and deafness, but Jackie proudly says, "Even with all these disabilities, today she is a happy, healthy young lady."

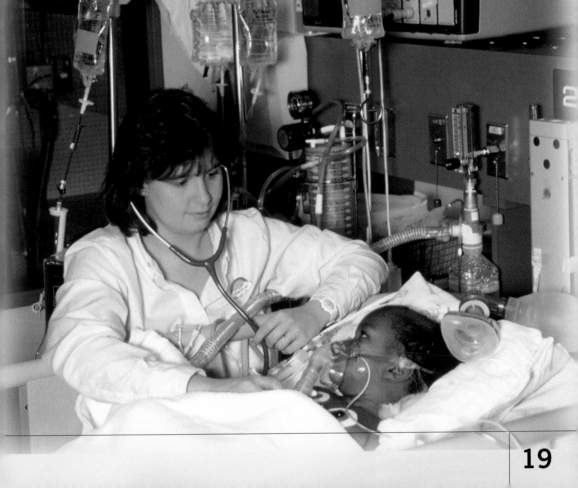

Hib meningitis

Hib stands for "*Haemophilus influenzae*, capsulated Pittman type b*,*" a very long name for a very small bacterium! Hib meningitis was once the most common type of meningitis in children under five in the United States, United Kingdom, and Australia. Thanks to the introduction of a vaccine in the early 1990s, it has become extremely rare in these countries.

Routine infant immunizations have meant that Hib meningitis is now rare in many countries.

The Hib vaccine is now part of the routine vaccination schedule for babies in many developed countries. However, in countries that do not use the vaccines, this type of meningitis is still common among young children.

Hib infections

Hib may be carried harmlessly in the back of the throat or may cause mild infections of the ear or respiratory tract (windpipe and lungs). Occasionally, the bacteria cause serious infections, including epiglottitis (inflammation of the epiglottis, the flap at the top of the windpipe), septicemia, cellulitis (infection of the tissues), and joint infections. They can also cause meningitis.

Hib meningitis has the same symptoms as the other forms of bacterial meningitis, though there is not usually a rash. Over 95 percent of children with Hib meningitis survive. In most cases, there is a full recovery, but after effects such as deafness, brain damage, and epilepsy still occur in approximately 12 percent of sufferers.

Who gets Hib?

Nearly all those who are affected by Hib meningitis are young children between the ages of three months and five years. The disease is unusual outside of this age range and is very rare among adults.

This is probably because between three months and five years the child does not have enough antibodies – special defense chemicals – to fight off Hib infection. Before it is three months old, the baby still has some protective antibodies received from the mother while in the womb. After birth, these gradually decline and the baby has to start making its own antibodies. By the time the child is five years old, he or she has usually made enough antibodies to be able to fight off attacks from the Hib bacteria.

If a person's immune system becomes weak, perhaps because of long-standing disease, then he or she may be at a higher risk of getting Hib again, even as an adult.

Viral meningitis

Viral meningitis is probably more common than bacterial meningitis, and it is generally less serious. It tends to affect children more than adults. The symptoms are usually mild. The person may feel slightly sick, perhaps with a headache and a raised temperature. Sometimes, the symptoms are more severe, like those of bacterial meningitis. There is usually no rash.

Antibiotics do not kill viruses, so there are no medicines that can be given to treat this kind of meningitis. Fortunately, most people get better with simple treatments, such as painkillers for headaches and anti sickness medicines for vomiting.

People with viral meningitis do not usually suffer the severe after effects that may occur with bacterial meningitis. And viral meningitis is rarely fatal.

Which viruses cause it?

Many different viruses can cause meningitis, but most cases are caused by just a few, including the follow:

- enteroviruses – these cause most cases of viral meningitis. There are about 80 different types, most belonging to two groups – Coxsackie viruses and echoviruses. These usually cause only mild illness.
- mumps and measles. The mumps virus in particular was once a common cause of meningitis in children. Now that most children receive the MMR (measles, mumps, and rubella) vaccine, this type of meningitis is rare in developed countries.
- herpes viruses. These viruses, which can cause cold sores around the mouth, sometimes lead to a mild form of meningitis.

In most cases, doctors never find out which virus is causing the illness.

The herpes virus that causes cold sores around the mouth can sometimes also cause meningitis.

Katie's story

Katie, a 30-year-old woman from the United States, had a particularly nasty time with viral meningitis. It came on gradually over four weeks. She remembers, "All I could do was lie in agony as my head felt like it was held in a vise. It came to the point where eating was no longer enjoyable because the nausea [sickness] was so awful. I was sick two or three times every day." Katie was eventually diagnosed with severe viral meningitis and spent some time in a hospital. After coming home it took her another four months to feel back to normal. She says, "I did get better, but it was a long and frustrating road with good days and bad days."

Most people with viral meningitis simply need to rest until they feel better.

Rare Forms of Meningitis

Most cases of meningitis are caused by viruses or by the three bacteria named previously. However, there are many other tiny micro organisms that can sometimes cause meningitis.

Tuberculosis

The bacterium that causes tuberculosis (TB), *Mycobacterium tuberculosis*, can occasionally cause a severe and often fatal form of meningitis. Children are particularly at risk in areas of the world where there is a lot of TB. In most developed countries, tuberculosis is relatively less common. TB meningitis usually affects the elderly, those with weak immune systems because of other illness, and immigrants who were born in countries with high rates of TB.

Fungi

Fungal meningitis is rare, with nearly all cases occurring in people whose immune systems are weaker than normal. Most at risk today are those who have HIV/AIDS.

Cryptococcus neoformans, the type of fungus that is most likely to cause meningitis, normally lives harmlessly in the environment and is found throughout the world. One of the main ways that humans become infected is by inhaling particles from dried bird droppings.

Protozoa

Protozoa are single-celled creatures that are considered to be tiny animals. One type, *Naegleria fowleri*, is a well-known cause of meningitis. It lives in freshwater lakes and swimming pools in very warm areas of the world, including the southern part of the United States and some parts of Australia. People can become infected after swimming or playing in the water. The organism goes up into the nose and from there makes it way to the brain, causing a serious (and often fatal) form of meningitis. Luckily, this is an extremely rare infection.

The tiny organism *Naegleria fowleri* may lurk in this lake.

Reptiles and salmonella

Salmonella is a type of bacteria that is best known for causing food poisoning. It can occasionally cause meningitis, usually in babies and young children.

One unusual source of infection with salmonella is a pet reptile. Reptiles, such as snakes, iguanas, and turtles, often carry salmonella bacteria in their intestines. These may then be passed on to people when they handle the animal. There have been many cases of children becoming ill after playing with reptiles. On the occasions that meningitis has developed, some children have even died. Washing hands after playing with pet reptiles is a simple and effective way of preventing the spread of infection in this way.

Who Is Affected by Meningitis?

Meningitis is not a common disease, but it can have such serious consequences that it is certainly an important one to know about.

Viral meningitis

It is difficult to know how common viral meningitis is. In many cases, people who get it are not sick enough to seek medical attention. It probably occurs more frequently than the bacterial forms.

Viral meningitis is more common in developing countries, where there may be a lack of good sanitation and clean water for washing. This makes it easier for viruses to spread from person to person.

Meningitis is common in places where there is poor sanitation.

Meningococcal meningitis

Meningococcal disease is said to be endemic – present at all times – throughout the world.

• The United States, with a population of 290 million, has roughly 3,000 cases per year. Since 1991, cases among young people ages 15–24 have almost doubled.

• The United Kingdom, with a population of nearly 60 million, has roughly 2,500 cases per year.

• Australia, with a population of over 19 million has roughly 650 cases per year.

• New Zealand, with a population of nearly 4 million, is currently in the grip of a long meningococcal meningitis epidemic, with roughly 650 cases per year.

Aboriginal doctors, such as these shown here, are helping to ensure that the very high rate of meningitis among Aboriginal Australians is taken seriously.

ʜʜWe are currently in the eleventh year of an epidemic that is expected to continue for a further ten years. There is no sign of the epidemic abating.ʜʜ

(Dr. Jane O'Hallahan, New Zealand Public Health Medicine Specialist, 2001)

Pneumococcal and Hib meningitis

Pneumococcal meningitis is the most common form of bacterial meningitis in adults. In many countries, such as the United States, United Kingdom, and Australia, it is the second most common cause of meningitis in all ages. In the United States for instance, there are approximately 1,400 cases per year. The highest rate of pneumococcal meningitis in the world is found among some Aboriginal communities in Australia, and is roughly 20 times the rate among non-Aboriginal Australians.

In the countries that use the vaccine, Hib meningitis is now much less common than it was. For example, in the mid-1980s there were about 13,000 cases a year in the United States. Now there are only a few hundred.

Who is at risk?

Anyone can get meningitis, but it is more likely to affect some groups of people than others. Different types of meningitis tend to affect different groups of people, but those most at risk are

- babies, especially newborns, and young children
- teenagers and young people, from meningococcal disease
- the elderly, who are particularly likely to get pneumococcal meningitis
- those with a weak immune system, including people with HIV/AIDS, cancer, or chronic (long-term) disease. People in these groups are more likely than others to get the rarer forms of meningitis.

Schools and colleges

There have been many outbreaks of meningococcal meningitis in places where young people live or work closely together, such as in schools, universities, and military training camps. In one case in Sydney, Australia, an outbreak was associated with a popular nightclub. Many colleges and universities in the United States and United Kingdom provide informational leaflets to new students every year. The leaflets explain the symptoms of meningitis and when medical help is needed.

Outbreaks of meningitis can occur in places where young people live or work closely together, such as universities.

Meningitis epidemics

People in some countries, such as in the so-called "meningitis belt" of sub-Saharan Africa, have a high risk of getting meningococcal meningitis. Here, meningococcal disease is an epidemic. Every few years, large outbreaks affect a significant proportion of the population in those areas. During an epidemic, as many as 2 percent of people may be affected, which is 2,000 people in every 100,000! Epidemics also occur in developed countries, but much less frequently.

The Hajj and meningococcal disease

The Hajj is the annual Islamic pilgrimage to the holy cities of Mecca and Medina in Saudi Arabia. Several million people from around the world take part, spending much of the time gathered together in large crowds. This allows bacteria, including meningococci, to spread easily.

There have been many cases of meningococcal disease among people who have returned home from the Hajj, and among their close contacts. In 2000, there was an international outbreak with 60 deaths, and in 2001 10 people died in the United Kingdom alone. Many of these cases were caused by a relatively new serogroup of meningococcus, W-135 (see page 17).

Hajj pilgrims now have to be vaccinated against meningococcal disease, including W-135, before they can obtain a travel visa for Saudi Arabia.

This man is being immunized against meningitis before going on the Hajj.

Newborn babies

Newborn babies are a special case when it comes to meningitis. They are more likely to get it than older children because their immune systems are not as well developed. The bacteria involved are usually different from the three that affect older children and adults. Newborn babies are more likely to die or to be left with serious after effects than older children.

Hundreds of different types of bacteria may cause meningitis in newborn babies. The two most common are Group B streptococci (sometimes known as GBS) and *Escherichia coli* (*E. coli*). These often live quite harmlessly in the intestinal tract and vagina of the mother. They can be passed on to the baby during birth or from other people's hands after birth. It is very rare for these bacteria to cause meningitis in older children and adults.

Group B streptococci

Group B streptococci infections of newborns have become more common over the last twenty years. For every thousand babies that are born, between two and eight of them will get a GBS infection. GBS are the most common cause of meningitis and septicemia in newborn babies in the United States and United Kingdom. Infection may start either just before or during birth (called early onset), or the illness may start a few weeks later (when it is called late onset infection).

Babies like this one, born ten weeks early, have an increased risk of meningitis.

E. Coli

Everyone carries *E. coli* in his or her intestines. These do not usually do any harm, but there are some uncommon strains that can cause disease. *E. coli* can be passed to babies from either the mother or other people who handle them. The *E. coli* can then invade the a baby's bloodstream, causing septicemia and meningitis.

Risk factors

Some newborn babies are more likely than others to suffer from meningitis:

- premature(early) babies, especially those who are born more than six or seven weeks early. The normal length of pregnancy —full term — is 40 weeks.
- low birth-weight babies. These are babies who weigh less than 4 pounds (2 kilograms) at birth, and especially tiny ones, weighing less than 2 pounds (1 kilogram). Most full-term babies weigh between 5.5 and 9.5 pounds (2.5 to 4.25 kilograms) at birth.
- those who had difficulties during birth. Sometimes the baby needs a lot of help to be born or may go for a short time without enough oxygen.

Treating Meningitis

Testing for meningitis

The diagnosis of meningitis is made with the help of a hospital microbiology laboratory. Two types of samples are taken — cerebrospinal fluid (CSF) and blood. A sample of CSF is collected during a lumbar puncture. This is carried out in the hospital by trained medical staff (if the patient is well enough). The doctor inserts a fine needle into the area around the spine and draws out a small sample of fluid.

In bacterial meningitis, bacteria can usually be found circulating in the bloodstream. A sample of blood is taken and is immediately put into bottles containing a special liquid full of nutrients to help the bacteria to grow.

In the laboratory

The samples are sent immediately to the microbiology laboratory to be examined. There are two main types of tests, microscopy and culture. Most hospital laboratories have a microbiologist available 24 hours a day. He or she will examine the CSF sample immediately through a microscope, looking for white blood cells and bacteria.

Normal CSF is clear, with no white blood cells. In meningitis, the CSF may look cloudy and contain many white blood cells that the body is using to defend itself. The type of white blood cells is usually different for viral meningitis than for bacterial. Sometimes bacteria are seen in the CSF. In many cases, the microbiologist can tell which type of bacteria they are just by looking. Viruses are too small to be seen in this way.

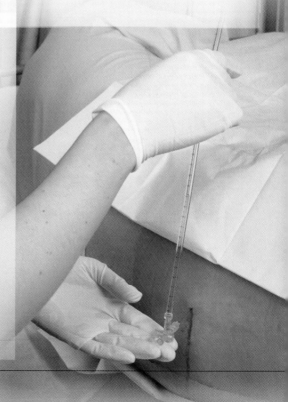

Here, a cerebrospinal fluid sample is being collected by a doctor during a lumbar puncture.

Whether or not anything is seen, the microbiologist will try to grow bacteria from both the CSF and the blood samples. He or she spreads some of the samples onto agar plates (agar is a special hard jelly that contains nutrients for bacteria). The plates are placed in an incubator, a machine to keep them warm so the bacteria can grow.

Rapid tests

Sometimes bacteria do not appear on microscopy or grow on agar jelly even if the patient has bacterial meningitis. This may be because the patient had been given antibiotics before the samples were taken. Many laboratories now have a range of rapid tests that can determine whether bacteria, even dead ones, are present in CSF samples. These tests use specially designed antibodies that clump together when bacteria are present. Rapid tests are not yet completely reliable, but are improving all the time.

A microbiologist examines body cells grown on the base of a special bottle.

The first few hours

For some people, meningitis develops slowly, over a period of several days, but for many it comes on very suddenly. This is especially true in cases of meningococcal septicemia, in which the blood is infected.

Symptoms can vary. Babies may become sick very quickly, and it is often not clear what is making them ill. Older people are more likely to have the usual meningitis symptoms, which include headache, vomiting, and fever.

Seeking medical help

Unless the symptoms of meningitis are very mild, most people will visit their family doctor fairly quickly. It can be difficult to decide whether someone, especially a young child, has meningitis, so admission to a hospital for tests may be needed.

If there is a rash, meningococcal disease will be suspected. This is a medical emergency, and family doctors usually stock supplies of necessary antibiotics just in case. These are injected immediately. The patient is then rushed to a hospital.

34

In the hospital

After arriving in the hospital emergency room, the patient with meningitis may need a lot of special care immediately. Fluids are given intravenously—into the vein through a drip— to replace any lost through vomiting. Painkillers may be given if headaches are severe, and anti sickness medicine may be required. Above all, the patient needs antibiotics. These have to be given intravenously so that they can get to the infected areas around the brain as rapidly as possible. It is likely that the patient will remain in the hospital for at least a few days, if not longer.

**Meningitis may be a
medical emergency and
the patient may have to
be rushed to a hospital.**

Hospital care

Someone who has a severe case of meningitis or septicemia may need special care in a hospital for quite a long time— perhaps weeks or even months. Meningococcal disease in particular can make a person extremely ill. He or she may need to stay in the Intensive Care Unit (ICU).

The Intensive Care Unit

The ICU is a special ward where extremely sick people are treated. There are many more doctors and nurses than there are on general wards. A lot of specialized equipment is used. People in intensive care often have several different tubes carrying fluids and medicines into their bodies. They are surrounded by various types of machines that monitor the body's functions, such as heart rate and breathing.

It can be distressing for the family to see their loved one, especially if it is a child, in such a strange environment. Although it can be stressful for the patients themselves, many say they cannot remember much about it. This may be a result of the medicines they have been given as well as the illness itself.

For someone with meningococcal meningitis and septicemia, the time in the ICU may be spent fighting for their lives. Many will recover, some completely. Others will have medical problems that will be with them for the rest of their lives. Sadly, despite all the antibiotics, special equipment, and dedicated medical and nursing care, some will die.

"The doctors let us touch his head and tell him how much we loved him. Our hearts were broken, we had lost our son, the laughter of our lives."

(John, from Maryland, whose son Sam died from meningococcal disease at age eighteen, National Meningitis Association, United States)

This boy is being taught to use his prosthetic arm after losing his limb to septicemia.

Serious after effects

Many people who are treated in a hospital for meningitis recover fairly quickly and soon go home to continue their lives. However, meningitis can leave serious after effects. Septicemia can lead to stiffness of the joints, arthritis, scarring, and skin damage. Kidney or lung damage may occur, and it may even become necessary for fingers, toes, arms, or legs to be amputated.

Learning to walk again after losing limbs can take many months.

Living with the Consequences

Some of the after effects that are a consequence of meningitis can be quite serious. Complications can occur with any type of meningitis but are more common after bacterial meningitis. About one in ten people who have meningococcal disease are left with disabling after effects. Pneumococcal meningitis and meningitis in newborn babies are even more likely to cause long-term problems. After-effects may include

- memory loss and lack of concentration
- clumsiness
- headaches
- deafness or hearing problems
- learning difficulties
- epilepsy (seizures)
- weakness or paralysis of part of the body
- speech problems
- eyesight difficulties.

If there are serious after effects, there will be a longer period of rehabilitation, or getting back to normal. The individual will need extra help from healthcare staff to fully recover. For some, this means many months in a hospital, which can cause real problems for family life, education, or employment.

Emotional after effects

For many people, it takes a long time to recover from the traumatic experience of having meningitis. This is especially true if the person had to be treated in the hospital for a long time. Young children may become clingy, throw tantrums, and may wet their beds at night. Teenagers might have problems later in completing their education, getting jobs, forming relationships, and becoming independent adults. People who have had meningitis can find that their moods change suddenly, going from happy to sad for no apparent reason. Many people say that they have good days and bad days.

For some people the experience of being so ill even has some benefits. As Chelsea (see quotation on opposite page) says, "I am changed for the better as I value life more, and realize my own mortality. I want to make things count."

People who are recovering from meningitis may need extra support from their family and friends for a while. Teachers and employers need to be aware of what a difficult time it has been for the child or adult returning after meningitis.

"When the teacher is talking and writing on the board and we are expected to listen and write notes at the same time, I have problems. I can do one thing or the other, but not both."

(Chelsea, sixteen, after recovering from meningitis, The Meningitis Foundation of America)

Kelly's story

Kelly was eleven when she got meningitis. Climbing into bed one night after soccer practice, there were no signs that a serious infection was brewing.

Kelly developed a fever in the night, and her arm hurt. In the morning, her parents took her to see the family doctor. He arranged an X ray of her arm at the local hospital. When she undressed for the X ray, the technician noticed black and blue blotches all over her body. Kelly remembers: "He got a scared look on his face."

Kelly was immediately admitted to the hospital, where she rapidly took a turn for the worse. She was flown to the nearest children's hospital, with her parents following by car.

In intensive care

Doctors in the Intensive Care Unit warned Kelly's parents that she was very sick and might even die. Her mom says, "There were tubes everywhere going into and out of her body and there were monitors and machines beeping all around. She looked so small and helpless. All we could do was watch and pray while the doctors treated her."

Finally, after fighting for her life for a week, Kelly started to improve. She was allowed to move to a normal hospital room. It was only then that her parents found out the name of the terrible illness that had almost killed their child — meningococcal disease.

Having meningitis can mean a long stay in a hospital.

Terrible after-effects

Although she was now out of danger, Kelly still had many serious problems to face and she wasn't able to go back to school for the rest of the year. The disease had damaged much of her skin, leaving painful wounds that took months to heal. One was so bad that her brother said it looked like a shark bite! Her doctors were afraid that she might never be able to walk properly again.

Kelly had many weeks of special treatment in the hospital, including surgery to graft new skin onto her wounds. Finally, she was able to go home again. Now, several years later, Kelly still has some problems, but things are improving. Her walking is back to normal — she can even run — and she is doing very well at school. Of her illness she says, "This is such a nasty disease that I am praying there might be a cure someday."

Meningococcal septicemia can cause severe damage to the skin.

Antibiotic Treatment

Antibiotics are medicines that kill or slow down the growth of bacteria, but not viruses. Antibiotics are the main type of treatment for bacterial meningitis.

There are many different types of antibiotics. Each is effective against a particular range of bacteria. Doctors prescribe antibiotics every day to help fight off common illnesses such as throat and ear infections. When it comes to bacterial meningitis and septicemia, treating them as quickly as possible with the right antibiotic can save lives.

How are they given?

Antibiotics are usually given as tablets or a liquid to swallow. However, this is a very slow way of getting the medicine into the bloodstream. Antibiotics for meningitis are given intravenously — by injection into a blood vessel — which means that they can immediately circulate through the bloodstream to reach the brain and meninges. The antibiotic most likely to be used in meningitis is penicillin. If the patient is allergic to it, another antibiotic will be used.

Early treatment

When someone has bacterial meningitis, he or she needs antibiotics as soon as possible. With most other infections, the doctor or nurse will take samples — such as blood, urine, feces, or a swab of a wound — before giving antibiotics. This is so that the bacteria can be grown and identified from the sample before they are killed by the antibiotic.

If meningococcal disease is suspected, there may be no time for taking samples. The doctor will probably give an injection of an antibiotic immediately, before admission to the hospital. This makes it more difficult for the laboratory to grow bacteria from any samples that are later taken from the patient (see page 33). In this case, that is much less important than immediate treatment.

Preventing meningitis

Giving a medicine to a healthy person to prevent him or her from getting a disease is called chemoprophylaxis. If someone is diagnosed with meningococcal meningitis, then an antibiotic, usually Rifampicin, is given as chemoprophylaxis to their close contacts, such as family members and any boyfriends or girlfriends. This is to prevent further spread of the bacteria and more cases from occurring. If there are a number of connected cases of meningococcal meningitis, then antibiotics may be given to other contacts, such as those in the same school or day care.

Antibiotics, such as Rifampicin (shown here), may be given to close contacts of people with meningococcal meningitis.

43

Vaccination

No vaccine protects against all forms of meningitis. Good vaccines are available for some forms of bacterial meningitis. For example, there is a safe and effective vaccine against Hib meningitis (see pages 20–21). Hib meningitis is now very rare in the countries that use the vaccine. Yet there are some important types of meningitis for which there is still no vaccine.

Military recruits in the United States are vaccinated against various diseases, including meningitis. Today, safety gloves are always worn by medical staff.

Meningococcal vaccines

No single vaccine will protect against all of the groups of meningococcus (A, B, C, Y, and W-135). A vaccine that protects against groups A, C, Y, and W-135 may be given to those travelling to countries with a high rate of meningitis. This is the vaccine that Muslims are given before they go on the Hajj to Saudi Arabia (see page 29). In the United States, this vaccine is offered to new college students and is given to all military recruits.

A new meningococcus group C vaccine has been introduced in the last few years for children and young people in the United Kingdom and has proven very effective. Australia also now uses this vaccine routinely for children. But there is no effective vaccine for group B meningitis, which is the most common form in the United Kingdom and occurs frequently in many other countries. Trials of a new vaccine in New Zealand look promising.

Pneumococcal vaccines

Two types of vaccines can be used to protect against pneumococcal meningitis. The first, an older vaccine, is effective but does not work in infants under two years old. A second vaccine has now been developed that is effective in this young age group.

In most developed countries, these vaccines are used for people who are at high risk of getting pneumococcal disease (see page 18). In Australia, babies from Aboriginal families, who are at an especially high risk of pneumococcal disease, are vaccinated. In the United States, all parents are now offered the new vaccine for their babies.

The developing world

Giving vaccines would make a huge difference to people in developing countries, especially those in Africa where many die in epidemics of meningococcal meningitis. However, many of these countries cannot afford enough vaccines. International aid organizations are trying to persuade the richer countries to help their poorer neighbors by making these life-saving vaccines more affordable.

Controlling an Outbreak

Over the years, there have been many outbreaks of meningococcal meningitis in schools and colleges. These usually lead to a great deal of coverage in the media. Sometimes, sensational stories can cause worry and even panic within the local community. In most developed countries, outbreaks of meningitis are dealt with quickly and efficiently by teams of experts in infection control.

These schoolchildren are being vaccinated during a meningitis outbreak in Cheshire, United Kingdom.

An outbreak in Wales

An outbreak occurred in the Pontypridd area of South Wales in the United Kingdom in early 1999. It started when a fifteen-year-old boy from a local high school contracted meningococcal meningitis and, unfortunately, died. Because it seemed to be one isolated case, the Public Health Department followed the rules for this situation and just gave antibiotics to his close family contacts.

Later that week, several more pupils from the same school developed meningitis. Others in the surrounding community also became ill, and one teacher from a neighboring school died. It was clear that this was a true outbreak and further steps had to be taken immediately.

An outbreak control team was set up. This was a committee that included representatives from the public health department, the local hospital, and the local schools. The team made the decision to give antibiotics to every pupil in the school — all 1,000 of them! The antibiotics were given out at the school on a Sunday, with healthcare staff working late into the evening so that everyone could be vaccinated.

By the time the outbreak was over, there had been thirteen total cases, and three people had died.

The media

Any disease that can lead to sudden deaths among children will cause fear and anxiety. Newspaper and television reports often add to this anxiety by deliberately using sensational language such as "killer bugs" or "deadly disease" and exaggerating the risks involved.

But when the media avoid sensationalism, they can play a very important role in educating the public about diseases like meningitis. One of the aims of the many voluntary meningitis organizations is to provide journalists with the true facts about this condition so that their stories will inform, not scare, their readers.

How Can Modern Science Help?

Meningitis has been the focus of a great deal of research in recent years. Most attention has been focused on three areas: vaccines, diagnostic tests, and genetics.

New vaccines

Vaccination is the only way to prevent meningitis. However, one type of meningococcus, Group B, has no vaccine. This is a big problem because Group B meningococci cause most cases of meningitis in many developed countries. Scientists are working on the development of an effective Group B vaccine, and in some areas trials of suitable vaccines will be starting soon.

Interestingly, there is one country in the world that does have an effective vaccine against their type of Group B meningococci — Cuba. Unfortunately, the Cuban vaccine does not work well in other countries. It does not protect against the types of this micro organism found elsewhere.

Diagnosis

People with suspected meningitis are often given antibiotics before they reach a hospital. In this case, it can then be difficult to find live bacteria in their blood and cerebrospinal fluid samples because the antibiotics have already killed them. More sophisticated tests, which do not depend upon the presence of live bacteria, are needed. There is also a need for tests that give rapid results to help doctors make quick decisions about treatment.

There are already some rapid diagnostic tests for meningitis. A lot of research is being carried out to make them better and more effective. In the future, it may be possible to discover which bacteria is causing the disease from a simple blood test.

Genetic research

In recent years, scientists have done a lot of hard work to map out the genetic material — the genome — of some of the important bacteria that cause meningitis. Researchers believe that they have found the complete sequence of genes of meningococci Group A (which cause epidemics in some developing countries) and Group B.

Determining the genetic make up of these bacteria should help scientists to understand exactly how the disease can be combatted. In turn, this knowledge should help in the production of new vaccines and perhaps new cures.

This research laboratory microbiologist is using a sterile rod to take samples of bacteria from a plate on which they have been grown.

Meningitis in the Future

In these days of antibiotics and vaccinations, it is easy to believe that infectious diseases no longer have the same destructive power that they had in the past. Meningitis, and in particular meningococcal meningitis, shows how false that impression can be.

Every year, even in countries with excellent healthcare, people die from meningitis, and many more are left with disabling after effects. It is important that this disease is taken seriously — that people learn about the symptoms and how important it is to seek immediate medical help.

The situation is improving. New vaccinations have made some forms of meningitis almost a thing of the past in some countries. Many children are now alive and well because they had protection against a disease that might otherwise have had severe consequences. And there are real reasons to believe that this success will continue as new vaccines become available.

"Our vision is a world free from meningitis and septicemia."

(The Meningitis Research Foundation, United Kingdom)

Increasing awareness

For the individual, the most effective way to prevent the severe consequences of meningitis is to seek medical help as soon as possible. It is vital that people know more about meningitis so that they can recognize the symptoms. This is one of the main roles of charitable organizations such as the National Meningitis Association in the United States, the Meningitis

Research Foundation in the United Kingdom, the Meningitis Center in Australia, and others.

These organizations exist to inform people about meningitis — its causes, symptoms, and treatment. They encourage and support further research into this disease. Many of them were set up by survivors of meningitis and their families. Their experiences affected them so deeply that they wanted to educate as many people as possible about meningitis. As Kelly (see page 40) says, "I try to tell as many people as possible how nasty this disease is and what its symptoms are, so maybe I can save someone some day."

Information and Advice

Many organizations offer information and advice on meningitis. They provide information for the media and encourage and fund research. These groups were often set up by parents and others who had been affected by meningitis.

Contacts

Meningitis Foundation of America
6610 North Shadeland Avenue,
Suite 200, Indianapolis, Indiana 46220-4393
(800) 668-1129
Website: www.musa.org
The Foundation offers information about meningitis as well as support for those affected. The website contains many true-life stories of people who have survived meningitis as well as those who were not so fortunate.

National Meningitis Association
22910 Chestnut Road
Lexington Park, MD 20653
1-866-FONE-NMA or 1 866 366-3662
Email: support@nmaus.org
Website: www.nmaus.org
The National Meningitis Association offers information about meningitis with a special emphasis on encouraging parents to have their children vaccinated.

Center for Disease Control and Prevention
1600 Clifton Road
Altanta, GA 30333
(800) 311-3435
Website: www.cdc.gov
The Center for Disease Control and Prevention provides general information on meningitis.

More Books To Read

Laskey, Elizabeth. *Mumps.* Chicago, IL.: Heinemann Library, 2002.

Routh, Kristina. *Epilepsy*. Chicago, IL.: Heinemann Library, 2003.

Peters, Robert. *Feather: A Child's Life and Death.* Madison, Wis: University of Wisconsin Press, 1997.

Willett, Edward. *Meningitis (Diseases and People).* Berkeley Heights, N.J.: Enslow publishers, 1999.

Glossary

amputate
to remove a part or all of a limb or other body part (such as a finger or toe) during surgery

antibiotic
medicine that kills bacteria

antibodies
protein molecules that are made by the defense cells of the body to fight off harmful organisms

arthritis
soreness and swelling of the joints

bacteria
tiny living organisms, some of which cause disease

cerebrospinal fluid (CSF)
clear, watery fluid that coats the brain and spinal cord

colonization
act of bacteria living harmlessly in or on another living organism, such as the human body

developed countries
term used to describe countries with many industries, a complex economic system, and a generally high standard of living —such as the United States and countries in Western Europe

developing countries
term used to describe poorer countries, such as those in sub-Saharan Africa, that are trying to make their industry and economic system more advanced

diagnostic tests
methods used by healthcare staff to find out which disease a patient has

epidemic
outbreak of a disease in which large numbers of people are affected

epilepsy
serious medical condition in which a person has seizures — brief periods of time during which they lose control of their bodies due to abnormal electrical activity in the brain

fungi
plant like organisms that may sometimes cause human disease

Hib meningitis
type of bacterial meningitis that particularly affects young children

HIV (Human Immunodeficiency Virus) infection
viral infection that leads to the condition known as AIDS

immune system
cells and organs of the body that help it to defend itself from attack by harmful organisms

inflammation
condition in which a body part becomes red, sore, and swollen

Intensive Care Unit (ICU)
part of a hospital where very ill patients are cared for by specially trained staff

intravenously
by injection directly into a blood vessel

lumbar puncture
diagnostic test for meningitis in which a fine needle is used to take a sample of cerebrospinal fluid; the lumbar region is the area of the lower back where the needle is inserted

membrane
thin layer of tissue that covers parts inside the body

meninges
three fine membranes that surround and protect the brain and spinal cord

meningococcal disease
term used to describe infection with the meningococcal bacteria, causing meningitis and/or septicemia

meningococcal meningitis
one of the main types of bacterial meningitis, a life-threatening infection that can be treated with antibiotics

meningococcus
common term for the bacterium *Neisseria meningitidis*, which causes a serious form of meningitis

microbiology laboratory
place where samples are examined to determine if they are infected with bacteria

microorganism
tiny living thing that may cause disease — viruses and bacteria are microorganisms

outbreak
sudden, eruptive occurrence – an outbreak of meningitis is said to occur when two or more people in a group (such as a school) or a small geographical area get meningitis caused by the same organism

photophobia
abnormal sensitivity to bright lights

pneumococcal meningitis
one of the main types of bacterial meningitis, a life-threatening infection that can be treated with antibiotics

pneumonia
serious infection of the lungs that can be caused by pneumococcal bacteria

protozoa
tiny, single-celled creatures that may sometimes cause disease

sanitation
safe disposal of human bodily waste and provision of a clean water supply

septicemia
serious bacterial infection of the blood, also known as blood poisoning

serogroups
slightly different forms of the same bacteria

sickle cell disorder
blood disorder in which some red blood cells are an abnormal shape

spinal cord
thick bundle of nerve tissue that lies inside the bones of the spine

spleen
organ that lies just under the ribs on the left side of the body and forms part of the immune system

sub-Saharan Africa
African countries that lie south of the Sahara Desert; the poorer countries in Africa generally lie in this area

tissue
mass of cells that form the different parts of the body

tuberculosis
bacterial disease that usually affects the lungs but may also sometimes cause meningitis

vaccine
substance that is given, usually by injection, to healthy people in order to prevent them from catching a particular infectious disease in the future

virus
tiny organism that can cause disease

white blood cell
cell of the immune system that circulates in the blood ready to defend the body against attack

Index